AONB MANAGEMENT PLANS

Advice on their format and content

Woolerton Truscott

Distributed by:
Countryside Commission Publications
Printworks Lane
Levenshulme
Manchester M19 3JP
Telephone: 061-224 6287

© Countryside Commission 1992
CCP 352
ISBN 0 86170 313 8
Price £4.00

CYNGOR
CEFN GWLAD
CYMRU

COUNTRYSIDE
COUNCIL
FOR WALES

COUNTRYSIDE
COMMISSION

CONTENTS

Figures

ACKNOWLEDGEMENTS

We gratefully acknowledge the help that we have received from a large number of individuals involved in one way or another with AONB management. We have found particularly useful the examples provided by existing plans, which have been liberally used to illustrate points made throughout the text. Special thanks are due to the Countryside Commission staff who provided invaluable guidance and constructive comment throughout the preparation of this document, in particular Richard Lloyd, Rosie Simpson, Ray Woolmore and Alex Wright.

Woolerton Truscott

March 1992

Throughout this document, 'the Commission' refers to the Countryside Commission and 'the Council' to the Countryside Council for Wales.

Background

Since the mid 1950s a total of 39 Areas of Outstanding Natural Beauty (AONBs) have been designated, occupying more than 13 per cent of the land area of England and Wales, and embracing some of the finest scenery outside of the National Parks. These areas vary enormously in their extent, landscape and wildlife resources, and in the nature and severity of the pressures upon them. What they do have in common, however, is that they all represent landscapes of national significance and there is, therefore, a national as well as a local interest in looking after them carefully.

A review of progress and action in the planning and management of AONBs over the previous decade was undertaken by Professor Smart and Dr Anderson, and was published in 1990. This work identified some measure of success in controlling inappropriate development within AONBs and in the promotion of schemes for landscape enhancement in a few areas. However, the review also revealed that action on the ground is thinly spread and has rarely even kept pace with the changes to the landscape brought about by agricultural, recreational and other pressures on the countryside over the past decade, let alone reversed the decline in landscape quality that has been experienced in many areas.

Financial constraints are clearly responsible in part. However, the absence in many areas of a coordinated approach to policy formulation and management within AONBs has limited the effectiveness of action on the ground, reduced the opportunities for cooperative effort at low cost, and in some cases served to exacerbate rather than resolve conflicts of use. The need for a planning and management overview of an AONB in order to reconcile conflicts and order priorities, together with the need to coordinate the efforts and activities of a multiplicity of land managers and users within an AONB, points to the conclusion that a good management plan is becoming an essential prerequisite to effective action on the ground.

Despite encouragement by the Commission, the review revealed that progress in the preparation of management plans has been relatively slow and the outcome variable. The Commission's new policy statement for AONBs, published subsequently, reiterated and emphasised the value of such plans in setting out positive policies and programmes of action to achieve AONB purposes. This statement was endorsed by the Secretary of State for the Environment in January 1991, and a revised edition was published by the Commission in October 1991.

The stated policy of the Commission, which was endorsed by the Council, is:

"to encourage the preparation of management plans for all AONBs, which are then used to guide and generate appropriate action".

At the same time, and in support of this policy, the Commission and the Council stated an intention to produce advisory material on the form and content of AONB management plans, drawing on the current experience of AONB and National Park authorities in preparing and implementing such plans. This document, which is published by the Countryside Commission and endorsed by the Countryside Council for Wales for the time being, is the fulfilment of that intention. It is hoped that its publication will assist, and also stimulate, the preparation of further plans of a comprehensive and consistent nature.

The scope of the advice

A review of a wide range of existing management plans and studies revealed considerable variability in format, content and level of detail, both of the issues and of the prescriptions for action. This variability reflects, to a degree, the intrinsic differences between AONBs but, more so, the fact that these areas are often at very different stages in the development of administrative arrangements and management programmes. Despite these differences, however, closer examination of the plans revealed similarities **in approach**, if not in detail, and these common threads have been drawn together in providing the basis for this advice.

The document is intended to be a 'user's guide' and is specifically targeted at the needs of the local authority officers who will be responsible for management plan preparation. Its purposes are principally:

- to provide a clear outline of the process and stages of management planning that translate broad aims into specific tasks — this will be common to all AONBs;

- to provide a logical and comprehensive framework within which the contents are organised, ensuring that all of the essential elements of the management planning process are addressed in a systematic manner — this should simplify the task of structuring the contents of the plan, saving the author valuable time;

- to provide a checklist of contents that covers the full scope of potential subject areas, including and supplementing those covered by the range of existing plans studied — not all of these will be appropriate to every AONB but authors may use the list as an *aide-mémoire* and select items that are of relevance in each individual case;

- to provide examples of 'good practice' and selected references that illustrate and may help to guide the process of management planning.

Beyond these principal areas, this document looks briefly at plan production, promotion and implementation. It is not envisaged that this document will in itself be used as a promotional device to stimulate the political commitment to plan production, although by its existence it may indirectly add weight to the case. Equally, the scope of the document does not include advice on specific management policies, although some suggestions are made as to the **type** of issues that may be addressed within different sections of the plan, together with selected examples of existing practice.

The advice is divided into two main sections: the first presents the background to the production of a management plan, describing the purposes, processes and approaches to the task; the second presents the format of a 'model' plan, describing the typical contents that may be included under each heading, and illustrated where appropriate by examples from existing plans.

Countryside Commission
March 1992

AONB MANAGEMENT PLANS IN WALES

During the preparation of this document, on 1 April 1991, the Countryside Council for Wales assumed the Welsh responsibilities of the Countryside Commission and the Nature Conservancy Council. The Council's remit combines those of the Commission and the Nature Conservancy Council, opening up new possibilities for a more unified approach in Wales to landscape and nature conservation, access to the countryside, and environmental interpretation and education.

The primary statutory purpose of AONBs remains, as yet, unaltered: to conserve and enhance natural beauty. But the Countryside Council is anxious that its broad and integrated remit should be reflected in AONB management and in management plans. It draws attention to the statutory definition of natural beauty as including flora, fauna and geological and physiographical features. The Council will, therefore, expect AONB management plans in Wales to give full consideration to all aspects of both landscape and nature conservation.

As the Countryside Council gains experience of integrated countryside conservation and management, it may issue further guidance on the implications for management plans, including those for AONBs.

Countryside Council for Wales
March 1992

SECTION I. INTRODUCTION TO MANAGEMENT PLANNING

I. WHAT IS A MANAGEMENT PLAN?

It is important to define what is meant by the term 'management plan' since it is used in a variety of contexts. The most familiar type of plan, as prepared by a wide range of organisations and, increasingly, private individuals is defined as:

> "a site-specific document prepared by the controlling owner, occupier or manager of a piece of land and which guides the planning and management of that land" (CCP 206).

This definition is not appropriate in Areas of Outstanding Natural Beauty (AONBs) where extensive tracts of land are within multiple ownership and control. Instead, management plans for AONBs seek to present an integrated approach to the planning and management of land in the countryside on a more strategic level and rely on cooperation and goodwill in order to be effective. In this sense they should perhaps be more appropriately termed 'management strategies'.

The difference, however, is mainly one of scale and means of implementation, the purpose and approach being common to both. The following definition is recommended, which may help to set the AONB management plan in context:

> "an advisory document that is prepared by, or on behalf of, all those organisations or individuals with a management role within the AONB, which establishes common aims and objectives of management based on a strategic view of the whole area within a wider planning context, and which recommends area-based proposals that will guide and stimulate management action towards the achievement of these objectives".

2. WHY PREPARE A PLAN?

The principal purpose of the management plan is to achieve AONB management, defined as:

> "positive action towards implementing measures for conservation and enhancement of natural resources, and for promoting acceptable social and economic development, including recreation" (CCP 295).

The plan is, in essence, the means by which the integrated approach to management of land is applied to a defined area. Moreover, the following purposes and functions can also be achieved:

- the plan can become a promotional tool, used to increase awareness of the value of the AONB and the pressures it faces, and to generate political and other support that will aid its implementation;

- the plan can be a valuable coordinator, bringing together the activities of a wide range of agencies and individuals, making best use of available resources and fostering an identity of purpose and collective responsibility for management of the AONB;

- the plan can present an opportunity to agree a set of common aims, based on a shared 'vision for the future' and on a well-researched and comprehensive record of the current condition of the AONB;

- the plan can provide a flexible working document that incorporates a mechanism for monitoring and review, allowing the reappraisal of objectives and policies in response to changing circumstances;

- the plan can provide a comprehensive approach, which is essential if priorities for action are to be decided.

Statements of intent or commitment

The management plan is intended to take forward and underpin preliminary statements on the role and purpose of designation and the policies for development control and management outlined within 'statements of intent'. The management plan does not **replace** statements of intent, which are still required for any new AONBs. Instead it reinforces and extends them by a more detailed examination of the key management issues, based on full landscape and resource appraisals, and cross-referenced to the development plans for the area. Where no statement of intent exists, or where one was prepared some time ago, the Commission and the Council now seek a reaffirmation of commitment to be made in the form of a 'statement of commitment', also to be incorporated within the management plan.

Figure 1. Guidance on developing statements of intent or commitment.

Introduction

The format of a statement of intent or commitment will depend upon its purpose and the stage of AONB management at which it is being prepared. For example, the Blackdown Hills statement of intent (1989) made a case for a proposed AONB and outlined what designation might achieve. The Sussex Downs statement (1986) was prepared at a later stage and includes a little more detail, while those for the Forest of Bowland (1985) and the High Weald (1988) are, in effect, the first stages of a management plan.

The role and target audiences for the statement should be identified at the outset. A statement of intent should be prepared for a proposed or recently designated AONB. For longer established areas, a statement of commitment is more appropriate. Some documents are intended primarily for internal use by the organisations involved, although consideration should be given to the benefits of producing a simple but attractive statement that may be useful for promoting the objectives of the AONB (eg High Weald). Sometimes other major interests may be invited to endorse the statement.

Proposed content of a statement

1. Introduction to, and purpose of, the statement of intent or commitment.
2. Purpose and implications of AONB designation.
3. Why the area has been designated an AONB (or is being proposed for designation).

This should include a description of the landscape quality that is to be conserved, the landscape character of the area and any special features that are most crucial to designation, with reference to cultural and historical aspects in addition to the physical ones.

4. Existing policies covering the AONB.

This should include those in structure plans, local plans and other relevant plans covering areas such as development control, conservation and recreation.

5. Problems and key issues affecting the AONB.

A brief analysis in relation to the main aspects relevant to the AONB such as: agriculture, forests and woodlands, development pressures, recreation and access, landscape and nature conservation, rural settlements and buildings, mineral extraction, archaeology and historical features, socio-economic issues, transport, eyesores, and other land uses.

6. Progress in AONB planning and management to date.
7. General outline of the action proposed to achieve AONB objectives, including, where possible, agreement that the Joint Advisory Committee (JAC) or equivalent body will have a right to be heard on planning applications likely to be detrimental to the AONB.
8. Priorities for action.

Source: Countryside Commission (1991) Areas of Outstanding Natural Beauty: A policy statement (CCP 356).

3. PRODUCING A MANAGEMENT PLAN

There are two principal aspects to be considered in preparing a management plan:

- what should it contain?
- how should it be prepared and used?

The following paragraphs describe the plan production process from inception to completion and use. The process may extend over a considerable time period and AONB authorities will be at different stages along it depending upon progress already made in management planning within each area. Seven stages are identified.

1. Promoting the need for a plan
2. Establishing an organisational framework
3. Preparing the first draft
4. The consultation process
5. Preparing the final plan
6. Promotion
7. Implementation

Stage 1. Promoting the need for a plan

In some AONBs the need for a management plan may already be acknowledged, often as one outcome of the publication of a statement of intent or similar strategy document for the AONB, as a result of a landscape assessment, or through the initiative of a Joint Advisory Committee (JAC). In other areas, it may be necessary to promote the need for a plan in order to obtain the required political support and the commitment and cooperation of all interested parties. It is essential to establish at the outset that the management plan is **not** just about local authority responsibilities: it is also about the future of an area of countryside in which many people will have an interest. Thus, a wide range of people who live in, work in, or visit the area and have an interest in its future should be encouraged to participate in preparing the plan and to assume 'ownership' of it.

The organisation of a programme of meetings of key organisations and individuals is probably the best way to raise awareness of the issues affecting the AONB, and the need for a management plan to help to resolve them. This may be supported by local exhibitions and the production and distribution of promotional material, such as leaflets or the more substantial landscape appraisal documents, among local residents and organisations. This exercise will represent the beginning of the comprehensive consultation process that should accompany the preparation of the plan.

Stage 2. Establishing an organisational framework

To be most effective, management plans should be drawn up with the involvement of everyone with an interest in the AONB. In practice, the local authorities will have a key role to play in preparing the plan and in coordinating implementation measures but close collaboration, through a forum for regular liaison, is essential to the plan preparation process.

The forum should be formal enough to give it the appropriate level of significance, yet be open, flexible and 'approachable' to encourage participation by representatives of the public. The Countryside Commission has long been advocating the establishment of JACs, particularly in multi-county AONBs, and the new policy of the Commission and the Council re-affirms the need for all AONBs to have a JAC or comparable organisation, to support and encourage the active involvement of everyone with an interest in the AONB and to coordinate management over the whole of the area. The JAC, and officer support through a Technical Officers' Working Party, would play a central role in coordinating the management plan production.

Figure 2. Suggested model terms of reference for Joint Advisory Committees.

Introduction

The JAC should support and encourage an active partnership between all of the agencies involved, and coordinate management over the whole of the AONB (and Heritage Coast, where applicable). The aim is to:

- ensure that the AONB is conserved and managed effectively;

- provide a forum for the exchange of information and ideas;

- consider any issues likely to affect the area adversely and agree action;

- make recommendations for new initiatives.

A range of organisations with interests in the AONB should be considered for membership. Members should include local authorities and the key organisations and interests, including representatives of local people, whose involvement will assist in implementing the management plan. However, their inclusion on the JAC is at the discretion of the local authorities. Ideally there should be between 10 and 20 members and, where it is not practical to include all of the relevant interests, regular consultation mechanisms should be established.

Brief for the JAC

The JAC should:

- coordinate the preparation of a statement of commitment and a management plan for the AONB;

- advise local authorities preparing structure plans, local plans or other plans covering all or part of the AONB, to ensure that policies and practices (including those for development control) are coordinated and consistent with the statement of commitment and AONB management plan;

- advise local authorities and other agencies on the level of resources required for effective AONB management and, where possible, manage their own budget;

- advise on, and coordinate the actions of, the constituent organisations to achieve the objectives of the AONB and, in particular, ensure that the statement of commitment and management plan are implemented and reviewed. This includes:

  —agreeing an annual work programme for the AONB officer (where applicable), countryside management service and other AONB project staff;

  —monitoring progress and achievements in implementing the statement of commitment and management plan, reviewing both documents every five years and producing an annual report;

  —carrying out special studies of key issues, as they arise, for example by setting up working parties or conducting research;

  —advising the appropriate local planning authority about any developments within or adjacent to the AONB that are likely to affect significantly the landscape character of the area;

  —acting as a forum for the discussion of major issues affecting the character of the AONB;

  —promoting other action that is necessary to further the objectives of the AONB designation.

Source: Countryside Commission (1991) Areas of Outstanding Natural Beauty: A policy statement 1991 (CCP 356).

Figure 3. Suggested job description for an AONB Officer.

The main duties are as follows.

1. To draw up (or where appropriate, revise) a statement of commitment and a management plan for the AONB in consultation with the JAC and others with an interest in the area, and prepare a rolling programme of work to implement the proposals.

2. To provide planning advice to the JAC on any development proposals that will significantly affect the AONB and communicate the views of the JAC to, and liaise with, the appropriate planning departments.

3. To implement the management plan according to the agreed work programme. This would be both directly, by coordinating and managing the AONB countryside management service and other staff and volunteers, and indirectly, through liaison with local authorities, land managers, voluntary organisations, local communities and others with an interest in the area.

4. To investigate and obtain sources of funding (including grant aid and sponsorship), to manage the AONB budget, and to produce an annual financial statement.

5. To interpret and present the special qualities of the AONB to interested organisations and individuals, including educational groups, local people and visitors, and to promote the objectives of the AONB generally.

6. To prepare an annual report and any other reports required by the JAC, working groups, constituent local authorities or funding agencies such as the Countryside Commission and the Countryside Council for Wales.

7. To maintain information about the AONB and to coordinate research into issues relevant to its management, for example land use change, recreation and access, erosion, landscape and ecological assessment.

8. To monitor the implementation of the management plan and to review it every five years in consultation with those with interest in the AONB.

It should be noted that some AONB officers will have joint responsibility for Heritage Coast areas.

Source: Countryside Commission (1991) Areas of Outstanding Natural Beauty: A policy statement 1991 (CCP 356).

The Commission and the Council also advocate the appointment of a specialist officer solely responsible for AONB work, to have general oversight of the AONB, to coordinate strategic development and management plans, and to service the JAC (Figure 3).

Organisational frameworks are likely to vary according to the existing administrative arrangements and size of the AONB. One such arrangement, proposed for the Wye Valley AONB, is shown in Figure 4. This arrangement is characterised by a two-way exchange of information and ideas with the AONB Officer and JAC at the hub.

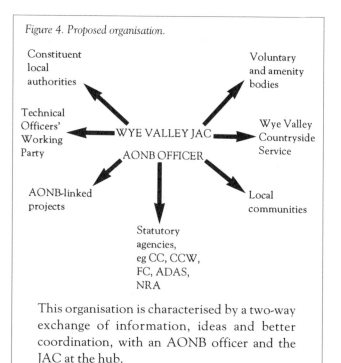

Figure 4. Proposed organisation.

This organisation is characterised by a two-way exchange of information, ideas and better coordination, with an AONB officer and the JAC at the hub.

Source: Adapted from Wye Valley AONB Management Plan 1990–2000. Draft for consultation.

The Commission and the Council also advocate, for some AONBs, the setting up of special AONB units under the direction of the AONB officer, supported by professional staff and with administrative back-up for the JAC. The unit would have responsibility for the preparation of strategic planning and management documents for the AONB, preparing programmes of work, coordinating their implementation and servicing the JAC, and would be financed by contributions from each of the constituent authorities, with grant support from the Commission.

Stage 3. Preparing the first draft

The first draft of the plan will usually be prepared under the direction of a senior (preferably 'AONB') officer, supported by other local authority staff, ideally through a Technical Officers' Working Party or as part of an AONB Unit. Where possible, such officer working groups should also involve other organisations.

> The *Gower management plan* describes the arrangements for plan preparation as follows.
>
> "The Swansea City Council realised that a meaningful and effective management plan could not be prepared and implemented without the cooperation and participation of many other organisations, landowners and individuals. Certain groups have a wider influence than others through their level of involvement and statutory obligations. For this reason the City Council invited West Glamorgan County Council, the Countryside Commission, the National Trust and the Nature Conservancy Council to assist in the preparation of the draft plan. These bodies had officers who were willing and available to participate in a working group on a regular basis during normal working hours. It is stressed that the function of this group was purely to assist in the preparation of the document which could be used for meaningful consultation with other organisations and the public".

Only certain key organisations will be able to be involved directly in plan preparation through these working groups. Consultation with other organisations closely involved with the management and use of the AONB should take place through the JAC, or other consultative body, throughout the preparation of the first draft. The cooperation and involvement of private landowners should particularly be encouraged, through the farming organisations, since responsibility for management, and therefore the successful outcome of the plan, is likely to rest principally with them.

The first draft should be for consultation and broadly adhere to the format suggested in Section 2. It should include strategic aims, objectives, and a range of management policies to be considered by the JAC and other interested parties.

It is not possible to provide detailed guidance on programming the preparation of a management plan as this will depend on the availability of existing data, the characteristics of the area, the complexity of the management issues and the staff resources available to undertake the work. It is likely, however, that for a medium-sized AONB a first draft would take two officers at least 12 months to prepare.

> The *Dedham Vale and Stour Valley countryside project management plan* covers an area of approximately 186 square kilometres, of which 90 square kilometres are designated as the Dedham Vale AONB. Following response to the publication of a preliminary brief, the first draft of the plan was prepared by a senior officer of Suffolk County Council, with input from other officers on specialist issues and with the approval of the JAC. The draft report was circulated to more than 300 organisations and individuals and the responses reported to the JAC. The revised document is nearing completion, approximately 18 months from its inception.

Stage 4. The consultation process

The process of consultation is a significant aspect of plan preparation as it is essential to obtain responses from a wide a cross-section of AONB interests.

The draft plan should be distributed to all interested organisations. To ensure that a grass-roots response to the draft proposals is also obtained, the AONB Officer and support staff should consider giving presentations to parish and community councils and amenity bodies, and holding small exhibitions in local libraries and village halls. There is merit in obtaining direct feedback from the public so exhibitions should be attended by professional staff if possible, and it may be useful to devise a system to allow the public to comment specifically on the draft proposals. This might involve the distribution of a simple questionnaire or form for completion and return in a pre-paid envelope. Press statements and conferences may also be appropriate at key stages of the process to reach a wide audience.

The consultation exercise should be planned well in advance, in some detail, and a programme devised to include:

- the preparation of a list of key organisations whose views must be sought;
- arrangements for public meetings;
- the production of exhibition material;
- the preparation of audio-visual aids;
- arrangements for publicity for events/meetings and distribution of information;
- arrangements for recording responses;
- a period for the collation and analysis of responses.

The consultation could take up to a year to complete, especially if each county or district feels there is a need for the draft plan to be considered in depth by Chief Officers before reporting to an appropriate committee, and a second draft may be necessary if initial responses require significant changes. In extensive, multi-authority AONBs the involvement of a Technical Officers' Working Party drawn from each local authority will be essential.

Stage 5. Preparing the final plan

The preparation of the final plan should reflect the results of the consultation exercise and the views of the JAC in response to the issues, and the advice of the AONB Officer.

There may be a tendency for the policies contained in the final plan to be weaker and less specific than those contained in the draft, as a result of lobbying by pressure groups or individuals. Pressure of this type is unavoidable but where a JAC has taken a strong line on a particularly delicate issue they should anticipate that considerable opposition may be expressed and be prepared to deal with it. As the success of the management plan wholly relies on goodwill, it is essential that criticisms are listened to and acknowledged, and that considerable effort is made to reconcile differences and negotiate changes. The JAC should be prepared to be flexible. However, every effort should be made to avoid a 'lowest common denominator' plan. Experience has proved that implementation work resulting from a sound plan is the most effective way to change negative attitudes.

Stage 6. Promotion

Target audiences for the plan should be identified and arrangements made for its distribution.

Everyone who participated in preparing the plan should be provided with a copy of the document and all accompanying maps and plans. Landowners with significant land holdings, and groups that showed little interest in its preparation, should also be targeted in an attempt to gain credibility for the JAC, the AONB Officer and for the management plan policies.

Extensive distribution of the final document is likely to be restricted by cost. In order to promote the plan among a wider audience, publishing a summary, in the form of an illustrated leaflet highlighting key issues and policies, can be a cheaper, 'eye-catching' and more effective alternative.

A summary 'broadsheet', promoting the management plan and its proposals, has been produced for the Quantock Hills AONB by Somerset County Council, on behalf of the Joint Liaison Group and with financial support from the Countryside Commission. The main issues, policies and implementation proposals are summarised and presented in an attractive 'glossy' format, together with a plan of the Phase One area. The broadsheet was distributed among district and parish councils, all consultees and commoners, and to the public through libraries and other suitable outlets. All 1,000 copies have now been taken, indicating the popularity of the subject and the success of this form of promotion.

A series of presentations to parish or community councils, amenity bodies, community and voluntary groups, for example, may also be planned to explain the contents and rationale of the plan, and a press release and local exhibitions can be used to announce its publication to the wider public.

Stage 7. Implementation

It is important to adopt and begin to implement the management plan as soon as it is completed. Clear and rapid progress on priorities identified in the plan will encourage support for management and perhaps begin to win over those who may oppose or be sceptical about the plan's proposals.

A well-prepared and presented plan should also assist in securing resources for implementation from the constituent authorities. It may also be an effective tool in promoting the philosophy of countryside management to potential sources of income in the world of commerce and industry. This may appeal to local businesses who are associated with a particular AONB and where many of those employed by the company live or spend their leisure time.

4. THE MANAGEMENT PLANNING PROCESS

The prescription of management action is the outcome of an analytical process that is common to all management plans irrespective of the extent or character of the land in question. There are seven essential stages to this process.

1. Stating aims
2. Describing the area
3. Analysis
4. Framing objectives
5. Prescribing proposals
6. Implementation
7. Monitoring and review

Stage 1. Stating aims

The broad aims of management are usually stated at the outset of any management plan and it is from these, and the results of survey and analysis, that more specific objectives of management are derived. In the case of an AONB, these aims would be of a general nature, reflecting the basic purposes of AONB designation and making clear the intended balance to be achieved between various conflicting land uses (within existing AONB plans an almost universal priority for conserving the special characteristics of the countryside is given). These general aims should already be set out in the statement of intent or commitment and would be reiterated here.

> The policies of the Commission and the Council on the purpose of designation are as follows.
>
> - The primary purpose of designation is to conserve and enhance natural beauty.
>
> - In pursuing the primary purpose of designation, account should be taken of the needs of agriculture, forestry, other rural industries and of the economic and social needs of local communities. Particular regard should be paid to promoting sustainable forms of social and economic development that in themselves conserve and enhance the environment.
>
> - Recreation is not an objective of designation, but the demand for recreation should be met so far as this is consistent with the conservation of natural beauty and the needs of agriculture, forestry and other uses.

Stage 2. Describing the area

A well-researched and comprehensive description of the area under study is an essential basis for management planning. However, the level of detail that can be provided will vary depending upon the extent and complexity of the area, the availability of existing information from a range of sources, and the resources available for undertaking new surveys. Suggestions for the type of base-line information that would be of value to an AONB study are made in later sections of this publication. The policy of the Commission and the Council supports the use of landscape assessments to provide a comprehensive description of the component parts of the AONB landscape (including cultural and wildlife aspects) together with an assessment of landscape character. The assessment should also appraise current and potential threats to these aspects and identify the type and scale of development that can be accommodated without a significant loss of quality. Broad recommendations indicating the type of management required to conserve and enhance the landscape character should be included. These would be developed further by the management plan.

Landscape assessments have been undertaken for a number of AONBs and typically take the form of attractive, full-colour publications that can also be used as a promotional tool. The following contents are those recommended by the Commission and the Council in their 1991 policy statement (CCP 356).

Suggested content for AONB landscape assessments

Introduction to the AONB landscape — physical and human influences and the general character of the area.

Features of the landscape — geology and landform, archaeology and history, flora and fauna, buildings and settlements, agricultural landscape, industrial features, trees, woodlands and forests, special features.

Variations in landscape character — description of the features and character of the main landscape types and how they inter-relate.

Perceptions of the AONB landscape — how artists, writers, visitors and local people have seen the area through the ages and what their impressions are today.

The importance of the AONB landscape — its distinctiveness in relation to the criteria for AONB designation; aesthetic qualities; what gives it a 'sense of place'; special features; prospects for change; implications for AONB management; importance in national terms.

Threats and opportunities — the main forces for change currently and in the recent past, and any trends within them. Implications for the future in the main landscape types. The scale and type of change that can be accommodated in each landscape type and that which cannot be absorbed without loss of character. Broadly what type of management is needed in each area to conserve and, where appropriate, enhance it.

Source: Countryside Commission (1991) Areas of Outstanding Natural Beauty: A policy statement 1991 (CCP 356).

Also to be included at this stage would be a description of the planning, environmental and management contexts within which the plan for an AONB is formulated. An appreciation of existing planning policy and management activity will help to identify factors that may influence management policy or implementation.

Stage 3. Analysis

This is a key stage in the process between description and prescription. It involves an analysis of the inter-relationships between existing and potential land uses and interests, identifying key issues arising from actual or potential land use conflicts. The options for management, problems and the opportunities, should result in a clear direction for management, a 'vision of the future' for the AONB that is held in common. This vision will reflect the overall aims of management and the particular qualities of the AONB noted in Stage 2.

Stage 4. Framing objectives

Following from the decisions reached in Stage 3, management objectives are then framed. These set out the areas towards which management action should be directed in order to achieve the overall aims. Objectives can be strategic in nature and likely to remain relevant over the longer term; or they can be more specific and apply particularly to a given area over the shorter term. Since the AONB plan has to deal with a very wide spectrum of issues over relatively large and often diverse tracts of land, the process of formulating management proposals is easier if strategic objectives are identified first (usually on a general, subject basis and applicable throughout the AONB) followed by more specific objectives relating to defined areas of land (on a zonal basis).

A typical example of a strategic landscape objective may be "to identify and protect those landscape features that characterise and contribute to the quality of the AONB as a whole and to the different landscape types within it".

In some existing AONB plans, strategic objectives are followed by statements of policy, which confirm the commitment to the achievement of these objectives and the means by which this may be pursued. This can help to clarify the mechanisms by which plan objectives may be achieved, and may follow on from policies expressed within statements of intent or commitment.

For example, the above objective would be translated into the following policy:

"the local planning authority will seek to protect the diverse character and quality of the AONB landscape and important features within it, through careful exercise of development control powers and by positive measures to encourage management and enhancement".

Stage 5. Prescribing proposals

The proposals are the recommended courses of action that are prescribed in order to achieve the long- and short-term objectives. They should give a clear indication of the management activity required but they cannot in all cases prescribe management to the level of detail that may be necessary for effective action to be taken. For example, proposals for habitat management may include general prescriptions such as coppicing of woodland or grazing of grasslands, but the detailed management regime to be followed, especially on complex sites, would need to be the subject of a separate site-specific plan.

The proposals may, therefore, relate not only to physical action on the ground but may also include proposals for further study in support of management objectives. Whatever their nature, they should be both comprehensive and comprehensible with the reasoning behind the recommended courses of action being made explicit, so that any person involved in future management understands the background leading to the decisions.

It is useful to indicate at this stage the likely scale of the proposed action in time and resources, whether it is a 'one-off' or ongoing management activity, an order of priority, and the likely lead agency for implementation and/or funding.

> Taking forward the typical objective and policy given above, an example of a proposal may be to "effect the repair and maintenance of dry-stone walls and hedgebanks, by use of countryside management services or 'other available manpower' in the following locations...".

Stage 6. Implementation

The implementation of the management proposals requires them to be translated into a detailed programme of action, itemising specific tasks, setting achievement targets and lead organisations, and allocating resources, manpower and priorities to each. This work programme will change from year to year, as will priorities and resources, and it is more sensibly produced as a separate document from the main plan so that it can be reviewed on a more frequent basis. Work programmes are discussed in more detail in Section 2.

Stage 7. Monitoring and review

The implementation of management proposals is only the end-point of the process in terms of translating general aims of management into action on the ground. Monitoring and review of this action, and of the management plan itself, is of considerable importance to ensure that the measures employed are achieving the desired results and that the plan is still relevant to the needs of the AONB. There are four aspects.

- Monitoring the achievement of progress and expenditure against tasks in the annual work programme. To this end, an annual report should be prepared for discussion by the JAC or equivalent body. Publicity of achievements to the constituent organisations and the general public should also be considered.

- Monitoring the extent to which this management effort has successfully contributed towards plan objectives, ensuring an appropriate concentration of effort across the scope of the plan. The level of activity and money spent in relation to the tasks in hand may expose an inadequacy of resources and the exercise may strengthen the case for future funding of neglected areas.

- Monitoring achievements in AONB management against resources allocated by the Commission and the Council, thus assisting the agencies in bids for increased funding and in targeting extra resources towards those areas of most critical need.

- Monitoring the **effectiveness** of action in achieving the desired results, involving an update on the current state of the AONB and a review of the objectives and proposals within the plan itself every five years. The implementation programme would be adapted in the light of this review.

Feedback in another direction is also essential. The plan will have been prepared within the context of county and district planning work and the objectives framed within the overall goals and aims for local planning. It is important that results from the management plan monitoring are fed back into any reviews of planning policies contained in structure plans and local plans.

5. THE FORMAT OF A MANAGEMENT PLAN

The preparation of a management plan must be approached in a structured way and the adoption of a model 'format' can help to organise the wide array of contents into a logical sequence. The format recommended in this advice may not be suitable for all particular circumstances but it presents an approach that is based upon the principles of management planning outlined above and which draws upon the collective experience of existing AONB plans.

The contents are grouped under five principal chapters, as shown in Figure 6 and summarised as follows.

Chapter 1. Introduction

This chapter provides the essential **descriptive** background to the AONB and to the management plan, setting out the overall aims of designation and the principal attributes of the AONB. The statement of intent would be used as a basis for this section and subsequent chapters.

Chapter 2. Contexts

The background is amplified by a description of the planning, environmental and management **contexts** within which the plan is formulated, identifying factors that may influence management policy or implementation.

Chapter 3. Issues, strategic objectives and policies

This chapter combines the **analysis** of the current state of the AONB and the identification of key **management issues** with the formulation of **strategic objectives and policies** for the achievement of the overall aims of management. These are AONB-wide matters, which are best examined under individual topic headings rather than on an area basis.

Chapter 4. Zone strategies and proposals

The strategic objectives and policies are interpreted within the context of individual management zones and are then refined into **area-specific objectives** and workable management **proposals**. An indication of resource requirements, likely lead agencies and priorities provides a guide to the **implementation** of these proposals, which can be used as a basis for detailed work programming.

Chapter 5. Implementation

This final chapter concentrates on describing the means by which the plan may be put into practice, including the administrative arrangements for coordinating management efforts, funding mechanisms, work programming, and finally the arrangements for monitoring and review.

In Section 2 of this document, the contents of each of these chapters is examined in more detail, together with illustrations of existing practice and reference to selected publications and other relevant sources of information or guidance.

6. PLANS FOR HERITAGE COASTS

Parts, or all, of the coastal frontages of 15 of the AONBs are also defined by the Commission and the Council as Heritage Coast. In total, 30 of the 44 defined Heritage Coasts include land within AONBs, and in a few cases, for example Northumberland and Isles of Scilly, the overlap between Heritage Coast and AONB is virtually complete.

Figure 7. Heritage Coasts in AONBs.

AONB	HERITAGE COAST
England	
Northumberland Coast	North Northumberland
Norfolk Coast	North Norfolk
Suffolk Coast and Heaths	Suffolk
Kent Downs	South Foreland
	Dover–Folkestone
Sussex Downs	Sussex
Isle of Wight	Hamstead
	Tennyson
Dorset	Purbeck
	West Dorset
East Devon	East Devon
South Devon	South Devon
Cornwall	Rame Head
	Gribbin Head–Polperro
	The Roseland
	The Lizard
	Penwith
	Godrevy–Portreath
	St Agnes
	Trevose Head
	Pentire Point–Widemouth
	Hartland (Cornwall)
Isles of Scilly	Isles of Scilly
North Devon	Hartland (Devon)
	Exmoor
Wales	
Gower	Gower
Lleyn	Llyn
Anglesey	North Anglesey
	Aberffraw
	Holyhead Mountain

Where AONBs contain defined Heritage Coasts there is a need to produce one of the following:

- a single management plan for the AONB and Heritage Coast together;

- a plan for the AONB as a whole and a second, more specific, management plan for the Heritage Coast areas of the AONB.

The Heritage Coast definition focusses on the particular management needs of coastal areas. These needs arise for two main reasons:

- coastal areas are often the focus for more intense visitor pressure, and a greater range of conflicting user demands than inland areas;

- the coast is subject to some unique issues that result from the interaction of the terrestrial and marine environment. These include pollution of bathing waters and marine litter.

The Commission reviewed its Heritage Coast policies in 1991. These are set out in *Heritage Coasts: Policies and priorities 1991* (CCP 305).

Objectives

The objectives of Heritage Coasts are complementary to, but wider than, those for AONBs. Heritage Coasts and AONBs both share a central objective of the conservation of natural beauty, and seek to promote appropriate and sustainable social and economic development. Heritage Coast objectives differ from AONB objectives in having a formal concern with facilitating public enjoyment and appreciation, by improving and extending appropriate recreational, educational, tourism and sporting opportunities where these do not conflict with the conservation of the resource. Finally, Heritage Coasts seek to maintain and improve the environmental health of inshore waters and beaches.

Heritage Coast services and committees

Most Heritage Coasts are managed by Heritage Coast Services, often reporting to a JAC. Where this situation exists, such services may be able to provide the basis for a management structure for the AONB as a whole.

Heritage Coast management plans

Management work on Heritage Coasts needs to be carried out in accordance with a management plan, and a number of Heritage Coasts already have such plans. Where Heritage Coasts are to be managed within an AONB service, policies for the Heritage

Coast areas — aiming to fulfil Heritage Coast objectives — should be included within the AONB plan through complementary but consistent policies, and appropriate cross referencing.

Heritage Coast targets

The Commission's policy statement on Heritage Coasts proposes a set of specific targets to be achieved by the year 2000. These targets relate to natural beauty, public enjoyment and environmental health, and will form a central part of Heritage Coast management and the core of management plans for Heritage Coasts. These targets could be an important component of the coastal aspects of an AONB plan.

The Commission is currently working with the Heritage Coast Forum to produce guidance on the planning and costing of the achievement of these targets. This will be available from the Heritage Coast Forum in 1992.

Figure 8. Heritage Coast targets.

The Heritage Coast targets are as follows.

Natural beauty

- The creation or retention of a strip of grassland or semi-natural vegetation along Heritage Coasts behind the beach or cliff edge, normally accommodating the coastal path, or where appropriate in the landscape, a field's width.

- The removal of eyesores identified in the management plan.

- The protection and enhancement of landscape features identified in the management plan.

Enjoyment by the public

- A continuous coast path along each Heritage Coast.

- All rights of way properly managed.

Environmental health

- Litter clearance and collection to be related to the highest standards for amenity beaches, as set out in the code of practice issued by the Department of the Environment.

- All intensively used beaches on Heritage Coasts to be designated as 'bathing beaches', complying with the European Community directive on bathing water quality.

SECTION TWO: THE CONTENTS — A SUGGESTED APPROACH

1. INTRODUCTION

This introductory chapter is divided into two main parts, both of which are concerned with setting out the background against which the plan is being prepared.

Background to the AONB

This section provides a summary of the basic facts about the AONB, which may not be available in one place elsewhere. Concise descriptions should provide a 'pen picture' of the character of the AONB, its special qualities, the date and reasons for its designation, and the existing arrangements for its administration. The primary purposes or aims of designation should also be clearly stated as a reminder of the balance between interests that the management plan is seeking to achieve. The statement of intent should be used as the basis for this section. These aspects may be considered under the following sub-headings.

General

This section could begin with a brief description of the concept of AONB designation, its primary purpose and policy directions, stressing the status of AONBs as landscapes of national significance requiring protection and management.

Specific AONB

Factual information about the particular AONB could then follow, such as its physical extent, the date of designation and any proposed boundary modifications. A concise summary of the landscape, ecological and other qualities that gave rise to its designation would also be appropriate here, although these aspects are given more detailed consideration later in the proposed plan format. The primary purposes of AONB designation in general could be expanded, if necessary, into a statement of broad aims for management of the AONB and will inevitably cover much of the same ground as a statement of intent.

eg The *Quantock Hills management plan* states the following three 'objectives' for the plan, of which the first two are really broad **aims** reflecting the primary purposes of designation.

- To conserve and enhance the natural beauty, flora and fauna and historic heritage of the AONB.

- To seek a balance of land uses in the AONB, maintaining or introducing agriculture and forestry practices where they contribute to the conservation of the area and benefit the rural economy. To accommodate recreational and tourist use only where consistent with conservation and the needs of agriculture and forestry.

- To provide the basis for a management agreement for the Quantock common land (as proposed in the Common Land Forum Report).

Administrative framework

Existing arrangements for AONB administration vary enormously and may be considered adequate in individual AONBs for planning and management purposes. In all cases it is probably useful to clarify what arrangements **are** in place, outlining the responsibilities for AONB planning and management, the composition and role of JACs where they exist, and the activities and administration of countryside management services for example. Existing arrangements for consultation and cooperation with other agencies, bodies and individuals (for example, by representation on Advisory Committees, Officer Technical Committees, or other fora) should also be described, although the roles of particular agencies may be covered better in Chapter 2 of the plan under 'Contexts'.

It may also be useful to indicate the nature of any perceived deficiencies in the existing arrangements as these can be taken forward by the plan, and recommendations made for improvements under the chapter on 'Implementation'.

Background to the management plan

For the management plan to be most useful it needs to be readily understood by the reader. It is necessary to set out clearly what a management plan is, why it is needed, what it seeks to achieve, and the rationale behind its preparation, so that any person involved in future management understands the basis on which decisions have been made.

Even more importantly, the ownership of the document must be made clear from the outset. The involvement of all those with an interest in the AONB in the plan preparation process will encourage a spirit of shared ownership and joint responsibility for its implementation. It should be made explicit that the plan is **not** a local authority document, and the arrangements for plan preparation, consultation and implementation must clearly acknowledge the vital role that a wide range of organisations and private individuals have to play in management of the AONB.

This section can be broken down into the following sub-sections.

What is a management plan?

Defining the terms 'management' and 'management plan' ensures that the role of the plan is clearly understood in the context of the AONB. The definitions given earlier may be used as a guide.

Why is a plan needed?

All AONBs are subject to processes of change and pressures imposed by human activity that may affect their special qualities. These pressures must be managed, as well as controlled through the statutory planning system, in order to reconcile conflicts and maintain an appropriate balance of land uses and interests to ensure the conservation of natural beauty. To be most effective, management should be directed towards clear objectives and targeted towards areas of greatest need. A management plan is the vehicle for doing this, as well as for coordinating the activities of everyone currently engaged in management of some kind throughout the AONB.

There is a need for a management plan in every AONB but the conflicts that it seeks to resolve differ from area to area. A concise summary of the nature of the obvious conflicts experienced within the particular AONB may help to reinforce the need for a plan. These will be examined in greater depth within each topic heading in Chapter 3 of the plan.

Ultimately, the purpose of the plan is to achieve the overall aims of AONB management. This general concept may need to be expanded in order that the full range of purposes and functions of the plan may be understood. Some of the many purposes of the plan were outlined in Section 1. The following example from the *Gower management plan* provides further illustration.

Figure 9. Purpose of the management plan.

The preparation and implementation of a management plan is the means by which the integrated approach to the planning and management of land is applied to a specific area. The control of land uses in Gower rests with a variety of public and private bodies, and numerous individual landowners and farmers. By agreeing and providing a framework within which future management is carried out, the plan enables any person involved to understand how and why decisions are taken, in relation to the reasoning behind the policies and proposals for action.

A management plan is able to serve all of the following purposes and functions:

- The provision of a well-researched and comprehensive reference record;
- the formulation of explicit objectives and priorities for management decisions;
- the establishment and acceptance of common aims;
- the identification of additional resources required and related proposals in support of grant aid applications;
- an assurance for continuity of management within the guidance of the plan and programme of work;
- to ensure the coordination of projects carried out by different agencies and to avoid duplication of resources.

Overall, the management plan provides a flexible working document and a responsive framework for action that will guide the planning and management of the area. This framework is developed in the context of overall goals and aims for local planning on Gower.

Source: Swansea City Council (1990) Gower management plan.

How the plan has been prepared

This section details the way in which the plan has been prepared, outlining the sequence of events from the passing of initial resolutions to the publication of the final plan and any interim drafts. The mechanisms by which representatives of landowners or land managers have been involved in the process should be clearly stated, and the collective ownership of the plan stressed.

> eg The summary publication for the *Quantock Hills management plan* stresses:
>
> "This management plan is not just an expression of the County Council's views. The County Council's main task has been as overall coordinating body, bringing forward the concensus of views and aspirations of all of the interested parties. It has been prepared on behalf of the Quantock Joint Liaison Group of members of the County and District Councils, who are firmly committed to the plan".

The results of consultation exercises on early drafts of the plan, or reports on public meetings or exhibitions, help to demonstrate the importance attached to the views of everyone with an interest in the area. The promotion of the plan's adoption and implementation, and the general arrangements for involving everyone in making the plan work, are equally important and are covered within Chapter 5, 'Implementation'.

The general stages of the management planning process may be usefully described here so that the approach and intentions of the plan are more easily understood by the user. A number of principles should be stressed, for example: the importance of following objectives and policies through to action on the ground; and the need to assign 'people to jobs' so that responsibility is taken for their implementation. The iterative nature of the process also needs to be stressed, emphasising the importance of continuous monitoring and review to ensure that the plan remains relevant in the light of changing circumstances.

2. CONTEXTS

Introduction

Explanation of the context within which the plan is written is an important part of the process of setting the scene for management and identifying some of the influences on its planning and implementation. This section should introduce the three different contexts within which plan policies must be formulated:

- **the statutory planning context** — which operates independently of the plan but which should acknowledge and reinforce the objectives of AONB designation;

- **the environmental context** — the existence of various forms of statutory environmental protection, strategic guidelines and national policies influencing activity within rural areas (eg agriculture and forestry policies);

- **the management context** — encompassing a whole series of activities that currently operate independently of a management plan, ranging from activities assisted or implemented by statutory agencies to the activities of individual farmers and landowners.

The statutory planning context

Statutory planning policy is concerned essentially with the development and use of land rather than with its management. However, an appreciation of the development control background to the AONB is essential to the management plan, so that it can interpret and take forward relevant policies and translate them into management action that will conserve and enhance the special qualities of the AONB. The management plan will not itself have a development control function but it should be complementary to the development plan system and at the same time seek to influence activities that are not necessarily subject to normal land use control (eg agriculture, forestry, countryside access, interpretation). It also provides an opportunity to identify the types of development that can or cannot be accommodated without significant loss of landscape character.

Planning policies that are relevant to AONBs may be set out at three levels — in regional and strategic guidance, structure plans, and local plans. It is unlikely, however, that they will be presented in an integrated way. Instead, they will probably be spread between several documents (especially in multi-county AONBs) and contained within sections relating to subject areas rather than to AONBs specifically. These policies must be brought together to provide a comprehensive picture of the statutory planning context within which the management plan is to be prepared. This may already have been done within a statement of intent or commitment prepared in advance of the plan, in which case the management plan need only summarise the policy background, highlighting certain issues of particular relevance to management as appropriate.

Any inconsistencies that may be identified as a result of this exercise, between the policies of different development plans or between statutory planning policy and the objectives of management, should be highlighted and fed back into the continuous review of planning policy. Indeed, a 'shared vision' for AONBs is needed at all levels of policy and action, but particularly in the structure plan, local plan and management plan context, which will mean interaction between the officers responsible for each plan.

> Professor Smart and Dr Anderson stress the importance of this two-way process of management plan and development plan policy formulation in their review of AONB planning and management (CCP 295).
>
> "In the general changing context of AONB conservation we can see great advantages in combining more closely the framing of planning policy, on one hand, and principles for management, on the other, in order to strengthen the connections and broaden the vision of both. The process should be an iterative one, in terms of both plan preparation and monitoring."

The environmental context

Environmental policy, which may constrain or otherwise influence the preparation of management policy for an AONB, is contained in a wide range of statutory and non-statutory designations, national guidelines and strategic plans. Other agencies with an interest in the countryside, such as the Regional Tourist Boards in England and the Country Landowners Association, also produce policy statements to promote the interests of particular groups. It is important to identify all relevant policy matters from this wide range of sources, and assess if they have implications for management planning.

Because policies are rarely targeted specifically at an AONB and are likely to be expressed in terms of a particular land use, they are best considered under a number of subject headings that reflect a more integrated approach.

- **landscape and nature conservation** — eg statutory and non-statutory designations, landscape and nature conservation strategies;

- **agriculture, forestry and rural development** — eg agricultural policy and support systems, forestry policy, minerals strategy, rural employment and housing;

- **recreation and tourism** — eg countryside recreation or tourism strategies, access areas, byelaws;

- **cultural heritage** — eg scheduled ancient monuments, historic landscapes, listed buildings, conservation areas;

- **other** — eg Acts of Parliament and byelaws relating to water company and Ministry of Defence interests.

It is the way in which these factors influence the management planning process that is of particular importance. Detailed elaboration of individual matters should, therefore, be avoided within the main text and included as an appendix only if this information is considered useful.

A checklist of relevant designations and other influences is given on page 21.

The management context

It is important in the preparation of a management plan to identify the range of agencies and individuals involved in land management, whose activities are likely to impinge on the management policies and implementation proposals.

As well as the local authorities, the Countryside Commission, English Nature, Countryside Council for Wales, the Forestry Commission, the Ministry of Agriculture, Welsh Office Agricultural Department and non-statutory conservation bodies such as County Wildlife Trusts and the National Trust, important groups of agricultural and landowning interests must be identified and consulted as soon as possible. The need for cooperation and the development of understanding between these disparate groups and for the coordination of management effort has already been stressed.

In many AONBs significant management issues are likely to be outside the direct control of planning legislation, and the goodwill of individual landowners will be important when the success of a programme of work depends upon obtaining the landowner's consent before it can be implemented. Examples of interested parties are shown on page 22. The list should only be regarded as a starting point.

When the specific involvement of each body or group has been established, an assessment should be made of their role in the AONB and reference made to existing management policy, plans or projects for which each is responsible. This information could usefully be included in an appendix to the management plan for reference.

Figure 10. The environmental context.

Examples of relevant designations and other influences on management policy formulation.

Landscape and nature conservation

International designations:

- sites that qualify under the terms of the RAMSAR Convention on Wetlands of International Importance;

- Special Protection Areas — sites that qualify under Article 4 of the EC Directive (79/409/EEC) on the 'Conservation of Wild Birds';

- Biosphere Reserves;

- World Heritage Sites.

Statutory designations:

- National Nature Reserves, Local Nature Reserves, Marine Nature Reserves;

- Sites of Special Scientific Interest;

- Limestone Pavement Orders.

Other designations and considerations:

- Heritage Coasts;

- Environmentally Sensitive Areas;

- Sites of county importance for nature conservation as identified by the County Wildlife Trust;

- Ancient Semi-Natural Woodlands;

- Nature reserves owned or managed by non-governmental organisations;

- 'Heritage Landscapes' qualifying for conditional exemption from Inheritance Tax;

- county strategies for landscape or nature conservation;

- Countryside Stewardship target landscapes.

Agriculture, forestry and rural development

- Less Favoured Areas, agricultural support mechanisms;

- common land;

- forestry policy, felling controls, indicative forest strategies;

- Tree Preservation Orders;

- Rural Development Areas (England only);

- county minerals strategies.

Recreation and tourism

- regional Strategies for Sport and Recreation (England only);

- county strategies for countryside recreation or tourism;

- access areas, byelaws;

- tourism development action plans;

- national guidance provided by statutory agencies, eg Countryside Commission, Countryside Council for Wales, English Tourist Board, Wales Tourist Board, Sports Council, Sports Council for Wales.

Cultural heritage

- Conservation Areas and Listed Buildings;

- Scheduled Ancient Monuments and other sites of archaeological importance;

- Register of Historic Parks and Gardens;

- areas of historic landscape.

Other

- comprehensive rural (or countryside) strategies;

- land under the control of the statutory undertakers, Ministry of Defence, water companies etc.

Figure 11. The management context.

Examples of agencies and individuals with an existing or potential land management role within the AONB.

- Local planning authorities as landowners and managers; providing countryside management and ranger services; management of access areas; financial support of management activities through management agreements, grant aid etc.

- **Countryside Commission/Countryside Council for Wales** through provision of grant aid and advice; promotion of land management initiatives eg the Countryside Premium for set-aside land and Countryside Stewardship schemes; negotiating conditions for Inheritance Tax exemption for 'heritage landscapes' etc.

- **English Nature/Countryside Council for Wales** as landowners and managers of National Nature Reserves; through notification and management planning for Sites of Special Scientific Interest, Local Nature Reserves and other sites of wildlife importance through statutory duties; provision of advice and grant-aid for management activities; negotiating conditions for Inheritance Tax exemption for land of outstanding scientific interest etc.

- **Ministry of Agriculture, Fisheries and Food/Welsh Office Agriculture Department** through provision of advice and grant-aid; administration and promotion of management schemes within Environmentally Sensitive Areas and other countryside initiatives (Farm Woodland Scheme etc).

- **English Heritage/Cadw** as landowners and managers of archaeological sites, monuments, parkland and historic buildings; through administration of statutory listed building and scheduled monument control procedures; provision of advice and grant aid for building and monument conservation activities;

negotiating conditions for Inheritance Tax exemption for land and buildings of outstanding historical or architectural interest.

- **Forestry Commission** through administration of felling licence controls; provision of advice and grant-aid for woodland planting and management under the Woodland Grant Scheme; management of Forestry Commission owned woodland; provision and management of recreational facilities etc.

- **National Rivers Authority/water companies** as managers of rivers and lakes and through provision and management of access areas and recreational facilities etc.

- **British Waterways, British Rail, Ministry of Defence and other statutory agencies or undertakers** as landowners within AONBs.

- **Non-statutory conservation bodies**, particularly the National Trust as major landowner in many AONBs but also RSPB, County Wildlife Trusts, Woodland Trust, Wildfowl and Wetlands Trust, BTCV etc; managers of reserves and sites; provision of access and facilities for the public; management of volunteer workforces etc.

- **Commoners and commons associations** as managers of extensive areas of common land.

- **Agricultural and landowning interests** as the most significant management influence; by their cooperation and participation in initiatives and response to influence of various groups and organisations eg NFU, FUW, CLA, FWAG etc.

- **Sporting, recreational and tourism interests** through their role in the provision of facilities and management of users and visitors within AONBs; role of Tourist Boards in promoting tourism and influencing the type and distribution of activity.

3. ISSUES, STRATEGIC OBJECTIVES AND POLICIES

Introduction

This chapter examines the inter-relationship between land uses and interests, identifying existing or potential conflicts, opportunities and the key issues towards which management should be directed. These issues tend to apply across the AONB rather than in specific areas, so most existing plans examine them on a **subject** basis.

The primary aim of AONB designation and management is to conserve and enhance natural beauty. Issues affecting landscape, wildlife and cultural resources are paramount and should be given priority consideration in AONB plans. Recreation is also important, and the health of the landscape can be linked with the maintenance of a prosperous rural economy. The plan should examine links between conservation and social and economic development and recreation, and identify opportunities for the promotion of sustainable forms of development or uses that help to conserve and enhance the area.

Using 11 subject areas, divided into two categories — conservation; and socio-economic development and recreation — the plan will cover the range of issues in existing plans. Although it may not be comprehensive or applicable to each AONB, this approach helps to analyse problems, opportunities and solutions for each subject area.

- **description** of the resource or activity, establishing its value and influence upon the essential qualities of the AONB;

- identification of the major **management issues** highlighting pressures upon the resource or the need to satisfy the demands of a particular activity for example;

- identification of opportunities for solving these problems by management (of vegetation, space, facilities, people, activities, traffic, etc);

- decisions on management options and priorities, made in the light of overall plan aims to achieve the correct balance between conflicting interests;

- translation of decisions into **strategic objectives** to direct management across the whole AONB.

- formulation of **policies** that demonstrate a commitment to the achievement of plan aims and the means available for pursuing them.

The conclusions and lists of objectives and policies for each section establish the framework within which proposals for action will be formulated in the following chapter.

Conservation issues

Landscape

The conservation of natural beauty is the primary purpose of AONB designation and the protection and enhancement of valued landscapes is clearly **the** foremost consideration in planning for management. An analysis of the aspects that combine to create each area with a distinctive 'landscape character', in the form of a detailed landscape assessment, is an essential first step in this process. Guidance on the content of such assessments is included within the revised policy statement for AONBs produced by the Commission and the Council. It may also be useful to refer to published assessments for guidance.

The assessment is then followed by an examination of the pressures that may threaten the character or quality of these landscapes. Typical will be the effects of changing agricultural and forestry practices on traditional landscapes; the pressures imposed by recreational activities and visitor numbers; and inappropriate or insensitive development.

The strategic objectives of management should reflect the desired outcome, ie the future appearance of these landscapes in the long-term. Policies derived from these objectives will be of a general nature, reflecting but extending existing strategic planning policy, and will remain relevant for at least the life of the plan.

The *Clwydian Range AONB management plan* includes the following landscape objectives, which are typical of other plans and of the level of detail required at this stage of the process.

Landscape objectives

- To identify and protect those landscape features that contribute to the character and quality of the area, including open moorland, stone walls, hedgerows, woodlands and limestone outcrops.

- To support and carry out measures designed to enhance the landscape, remove eyesores and repair damage, and where possible to encourage the reinstatement of areas reclaimed for agriculture.

- To encourage the retention of a diverse agricultural landscape.

- To support measures that increase public awareness and appreciation of the landscape.

Where possible, an indication of the likely lead agency for implementation and an order of priority should be provided.

References and sources of information

There has been a plethora of material published on the subject of landscape assessment which is summarised in a report by the Landscape Research Group for the Countryside Commission. There is at present no definitive method but the Countryside Commission's approach (CCD 18) provides a concise technique and the approach in the Warwickshire Landscapes Project (CCP 332) is particularly helpful in predominantly lowland areas. The *Arden landscape guidelines* published by Warwickshire County Council (1991) show how land management guidelines can be developed for a landscape assessment. Recent landscape assessments for AONBs are listed below together with other references that may be of value.

Countryside Commission (1987) *Landscape assessment: A Countryside Commission approach*, CCD 18

Countryside Commission (1987) *The New Forest landscape*, CCP 220

Countryside Commission (1988) *Landscape assessment of farmland*, CCP 225

Countryside Commission (1988) *A review of recent practice and research in landscape assessment*, CCD 25

Countryside Commission (1989) *The Blackdown Hills landscape*, CCP 258

Countryside Commission (1990) *The Cambrian Mountains landscape*, CCP 293

Countryside Commission (1990) *The Cotswold landscape*, CCP 294

Countryside Commission (1991) *Assessment and conservation of landscape character: The Warwickshire Landscapes Project approach*, CCP 332

Countryside Commission (1991) *The East Hampshire landscape*, CCP 358

Countryside Commission (1991) *Nidderdale Landscape*, CCP 330

Countryside Commission (1991) *North Pennines landscape*, CCP 318

Lovejoy, D. (ed) (1979) *Land use and landscape planning* 2nd Edition, Leonard Hill

Nature conservation

The flora, fauna, geological and physiographic features that make up the natural heritage of an AONB are part and parcel of its 'natural beauty'. This natural heritage affects not only the appearance and health of our valued landscapes, providing aesthetic and inspirational value, but also provides an important scientific, educational and recreational resource as well as having an intrinsic value in its own right. Nature conservation is therefore an essential consideration in AONB management.

As with landscape, an important first step in the formulation of management policy is to describe the resource and identify the features of value. The most valuable sites will be apparent from their designation as SSSIs or nature reserves but non-statutory sites of regional, county or local importance should also be recognised for their worth, as indeed should wildlife habitats and all features in the landscape, however small-scale, that contribute to the natural heritage. Apart from listing those areas covered by some form of designation, it may be useful to divide the AONB into principal habitat groups: eg inter-tidal areas, saltmarsh, sand dunes, limestone grassland, acid grassland, lowland heath, woodlands etc. Where available, basic habitat surveys, such as the NCC Phase 1 ecological survey, would assist with this breakdown. More detailed surveys of individual habitats (possibly using the recently developed National Vegetation Classification) will provide further information on which to base evaluations of nature conservation importance. Information regarding the range and quality of habitats within the AONB may not be available, however, and in these circumstances a key policy of the plan should be to encourage the undertaking of necessary surveys and evaluations, and the collation of all existing data. The occurrence of rare or specially protected species may also be relevant.

General pressures affecting nature conservation interests and those specific to different habitat groups may then be described. Such pressures will include absence of management; damaging agricultural practices; disturbance by recreational activity or visitor pressure; development pressure etc.

Typical objectives for nature conservation are given by the *Gower management plan*:

2.12 To ensure the protection of National Nature Reserves, SSSIs and Local Nature Reserves throughout the Peninsula.

2.13 To promote the adoption of appropriate schemes of management for such sites as well as for other areas of significant natural history interest. In particular to promote in conjunction with local commons management committees appropriate schemes of management for common land that contributes substantially to the maintenance of the existing nature conservation interests of such areas. To continue to promote schemes of woodland management designed to improve such areas for wildlife conservation.

2.14 To safeguard areas of local interest for their geology, landforms, flora and fauna and otherwise to ensure that agriculture, recreation, tourism and other developments do not prejudice the primary landscape and nature interest of Gower for which the Peninsula is justly famed.

2.15 To support and in addition carry out measures designed to enhance the landscape and wildlife of Gower.

2.16 To initiate control of invasive and alien plant species that threaten the native character of Gower.

2.17 To seek measures and agreements for the control of bait digging and shell-fishing at levels that do not prejudice the long-term survival of stock.

References and sources of information

The following organisations are likely to hold varying amounts of data on the type, extent and quality of wildlife resources within the AONB.

- English Nature/Countryside Council for Wales
- County Wildlife Trusts
- Royal Society for the Protection of Birds
- Wildfowl and Wetlands Trust
- British Trust for Ornithology
- National Trust
- Forestry Commission

Biological Data Banks (held by County Museums or Ecological Advisory Services)

Countryside Commission (1990) *Countryside and nature conservation issues in district local plans, CCP 317*

English Nature (in prep) *Nature conservation strategies and development plans*

Nature Conservancy Council (1983) *Handbook for the preparation of management plans*

Nature Conservancy Council (1984) *Nature conservation in Great Britain*

Nature Conservancy Council (1988) *Guidelines for the selection of Sites of Special Scientific Interest*

Nature Conservancy Council (1988) *Site management plans for nature conservation — a working guide*

Ratcliffe, D.A. (1987) *A nature conservation review*, Cambridge University Press

While strategic objectives should be reflected in general management policies for these habitats or designated areas under individual zone studies, it is inappropriate to include detailed management prescriptions for habitats/vegetation types or sites within the plan. Where these are required, their preparation should be recommended by the AONB plan and undertaken independently of it by the appropriate body as a means of achieving plan objectives.

Of course, many organisations (notably English Nature and the Countryside Council for Wales, RSPB and County Wildlife Trusts) will already be prescribing and undertaking management on land within the AONB towards nature conservation objectives, and the AONB plan should acknowledge and complement these efforts.

Lead agencies and priorities should be indicated where possible.

Cultural heritage

This heading embraces all of the historical sites and features that contribute towards our cultural heritage. These include archaeological sites/ancient monuments, listed buildings, conservation areas and other historic buildings or features worthy of protection but which do not come under any statutory control. These features are critical both to the appearance and character of the AONB in many areas and also provide an invaluable record of the way in which the landscape has evolved over time. They are also increasingly the focus of public interest.

English Heritage has recently published a consultation draft of a document on the identification and assessment of historic landscape, and intends in due course to promote the better identification and management of nationally important historic landscapes, many of which are likely to fall within AONBs.

A full description of the resource is the key to planning for management, and if this information is not currently available it should be a recommendation of the plan that the database is improved. It is also necessary to attempt to quantify the contribution that particular components of the cultural landscape (whether built features such as farm buildings and field walls, or less tangible features such as field systems, settlements and past land use) make to the AONB's landscape character.

The main issues affecting heritage sites are likely to include inappropriate development; agricultural damage; lack of management; vulnerability of the site to visitor pressure; and the need for, and appropriateness of, interpretation.

Strategic objectives and policies should be stated, but more detailed prescriptions for individual sites should be covered either within the zone-based section of the plan or, if very detailed, within a separate site-based management document. Lead agencies and priorities should be identified.

References and sources of information
Data on the cultural heritage are mainly held by local authorities, generally at district level for historic buildings and conservation areas, and by county council archaeological officers for archaeological sites (the County Sites and Monuments Records). Further information can be obtained from English Heritage and Cadw in Wales (principally for their own landholdings but also for scheduled monuments) or from heritage landowners such as the National Trust.

Darvill, T. (1987) *Ancient monuments in the countryside: An archaeological management review*, English Heritage Archaeological Report No 5. See in particular its full bibliography of archaeological management information.

Department of the Environment/Welsh Office Planning Policy Guidance Notes (1990) *Archaeology and planning*, PPG 16

English Heritage (1990) *Conversion of historic farm buildings*

Socio-economic issues

The priorities for management lie with the conservation and enhancement of the natural and cultural heritage of the AONB, and the policies identified earlier concentrate on finding ways of resolving conflicts of use and identifying opportunities to the benefit of the environment. It is also important, however, to look at the needs of visitors, of the local community and of the health of the rural economy in general for its own sake and partly because of the spin-offs for the environment that are very often the outcome of rural prosperity.

The purpose of this section should be to identify opportunities for management that promote socio-economic interests, where compatible with overriding conservation objectives, and provide for recreation.

Agriculture

In every AONB, farming has had a fundamental part to play in the development of the landscape. It is also an essential part of community life and still provides a high proportion of jobs in many rural areas. It should be the aim of the management plan to promote and encourage measures that will reconcile the objectives of landscape and nature conservation with the need to maintain a healthy farming economy.

The best way to conserve the farmed landscape is through traditional farming, but at present farmers in most sectors face an uncertain future. The plan should consider the likely consequences of future structural changes in agriculture and identify the problems and opportunities that may result.

Assistance, through conservation advice, grant aid for conservation work, management agreements, or agreements under the Countryside Stewardship scheme, will be needed and could be promoted by the plan. Countryside management can also greatly assist farmers in some areas by helping them with practical management and relieving them of problems created by visitors.

Opportunities for diversification and the provision of alternative farm incomes should also be identified and promoted by the plan where they would not conflict with landscape or nature conservation objectives, eg the re-use of redundant agricultural buildings by appropriate development. In some cases there may be spin-offs from development of this kind in the form of a return commitment to the conservation management of other landscape, wildlife or historic features.

Opportunities for joint initiatives between the local authority, the Rural Development Commission, the Welsh Development Agency, the Development Board for Rural Wales and other relevant bodies may be recommended, which aim to integrate social, economic and environmental interests in solving problems arising from changes in the farming economy.

The management plan should also touch upon such issues as the siting and design of new agricultural buildings and access roads where the arrangements for notifying planning authorities of such proposals and the discretionary planning control that have applied in National Parks for some years are being extended throughout the countryside.

References and sources of information

The changing emphasis on 'environmentally friendly' farming is reflected in a number of recent initiatives aimed at encouraging less intensive management of agricultural land. The situation is changing rapidly but those of relevance currently include:

- Environmentally Sensitive Areas (information from the Ministry of Agriculture, Fisheries and Food/Welsh Office Agriculture Department)

- Set-aside, including in a selected area the Countryside Premium for set-aside land (information from MAFF, WOAD, Countryside Commission)

- Countryside Stewardship (information from the Countryside Commission)

- Tir Cymen — a farmland stewardship scheme in Wales (information from the Countryside Council for Wales)

- English Heritage (1990) Conversion of historic farm buildings.

Advice on management of agricultural land is given by ADAS or WOAD and county Farming and Wildlife Advisory Groups. Information on land management issues may be obtained from the National Farmers' Union, Farmers Union of Wales, Country Landowners' Association and Moorland Association.

Countryside Commission and Nature Conservancy Council (1989) *The Countryside Premium for set-aside land*, CCP 267

Countryside Commission (1989) *Incentives for a new direction for farming*, CCP 262

Countryside Commission (1990) *The North Pennines AONB: Grants and advice available for conservation and development*, CCP 290

Countryside Commission (1990) *The North Pennines AONB: Issues and priorities*, CCP 289

Countryside Commission (1991) *Countryside Stewardship: An outline of the Countryside Commission proposals*, CCP 346

Countryside Council for Wales (1991) *Tir Cymen — a farmland stewardship scheme in Wales*, News Release 22 October 1991

Ministry of Agriculture, Fisheries and Food (1989) *Environmentally Sensitive Areas: First report*, HMSO London

National Farmers' Union (1990) *Land use policy review: Interim report*

Royal Society for the Protection of Birds (1988) *The reform of the Common Agricultural Policy: New opportunities for wildlife and the environment — discussion paper*

Forestry and woodlands

The value of woodlands in the landscape and as wildlife habitats will have been addressed in previous sections, mainly in the context of the conservation of important examples. Opportunities also exist for the management of plantations and creation of new woodlands, for timber production and for landscape, wildlife and recreation. Based on landscape and nature conservation assessments, together with an assessment of the present extent, nature and use of the existing woodland resource within the AONB, strategic objectives may seek to encourage new plantings, of a range of appropriate types and uses, and encourage management of the existing stock to provide opportunities for wildlife, recreation and commercial timber production. In this context, indicative forestry strategies can provide an excellent vehicle for creative landscape conservation. The approach, developed in Scotland, is being modified for use in England and Wales, where the Commission has supported the preparation of strategies for Buckinghamshire and the Cambrian Mountains.

Typical objectives usually include measures to promote management of new and existing woodlands through various financial mechanisms, and to achieve a balance between commercial, landscape and nature conservation objectives. The *Gower management plan* specifically proposes the zoning of woodlands in accordance with the following priorities:

- nature reserves — nature conservation will have priority but timber production should be accepted where compatible with this function;

- commercial woodlands — primarily managed for a renewable crop of native broadleaves and nature conservation;

- recreational woodlands — managed to provide a broadleaved woodland with facilities for visitors and wildlife habitats;

- natural woodlands — non-commercial woodlands that should be maintained as native broadleaved woodlands in perpetuity; grazing should be prevented and existing public access should be maintained and improved where necessary; it is desirable that large blocks should eventually become nature reserves or recreational woodlands;

- ornamental woodlands — these are formal parklands or 'embellished' natural woodlands that should be retained as formal ornamental areas with new planting of native and exotic species as necessary.

References and sources of information

The main sources of information on the extent, type and condition of woodlands within the AONB will be the Forestry Commission and also conservation bodies such as English Nature, Countryside Council for Wales, Coed Cymru (in Wales), County Wildlife Trusts and the National Trust. The information may range from a basic inventory of the resource to detailed surveys of individual woods. These bodies, and also the Countryside Commission, will have views on forestry policy within the AONB that should assist in the preparation of forestry and woodland strategies.

Countryside Commission (1983) *Small woods on farms*, CCP 143

Countryside Commission (1985) *Cooperation and farm woodland management*, CCP 191

Countryside Commission (1987) *Forestry in the countryside*, CCP 245

Nature Conservancy Council (1986) *Nature conservation and afforestation*

Nature Conservancy Council (various) Provisional inventories of ancient woodland, produced for all counties

Scottish Development Department (13/1990) *Indicative forestry strategies*

Tourism

Tourism is likely to make a significant, if not vital, contribution to the economy of many AONBs. The creation of jobs and strengthening of the local economy by the promotion of tourism needs to be balanced against the protection of the environmental qualities that form the basic attraction to visitors.

The management plan should first examine the level and distribution of tourist activity and the contribution that this currently makes to the rural economy. This will involve the collation of data on visitor numbers, patterns of activities, seasonal variations, trends etc, together with information regarding employment and other tourism-related spin-offs to the local economy.

An analysis of the impact of current levels of activity on landscape and wildlife resources will identify the extent to which it is compatible with conservation objectives. In areas where a decline in environmental quality has resulted, policies should be aimed at reducing levels of pressure or managing existing pressures more effectively. In other, more robust, areas tourism development may be more appropriate, and in some cases positively encouraged. In all cases, the emphasis should be on the provision of visitor facilities that do not prejudice the inherent environmental qualities of the area, and opportunities for the development of 'green tourism' should be promoted.

Policies need to reflect and complement existing tourism strategies and identify opportunities for collaborative initiatives, for example through Tourism Development Action Programmes. These may involve the English or Wales Tourist Boards, Regional Tourist Boards, the Rural Development Commission, Development Board for Rural Wales or Welsh Development Agency, local authorities, the Countryside Commission or the Countryside Council for Wales, and seek to promote tourism development in a coordinated and sensitive manner.

As the result of a seminar held in 1989, the English Tourist Board, the Rural Development Commission, and the local authorities have set up the North Pennines Tourism Partnership whose aim is to promote green tourism within the AONB. The emphasis is on the marketing of the AONB as a recognisable entity and improving the range and standard of facilities and attractions, and on encouraging community support for projects in return for the provision of advice and financial backing for community life itself.

References and sources of information

Local authorities are already active in promoting tourism, and county or even district strategies or tourism development action programmes may exist in a number of counties. The English and Wales Tourist Boards, the Regional Tourist Boards in England, the Countryside Commission and the Countryside Council for Wales are the other principal sources of information and guidance on tourism-related issues.

Countryside Commission (1990) *The North Pennines AONB: Grants for conservation and rural development*, CCP 290

Countryside Commission (1990) *The North Pennines AONB: Issues and priorities*, CCP 289

Countryside Commission and English Tourist Board (1989) *Principles for tourism in the countryside*

English Tourist Board (1988) *Visitors in the countryside: Rural tourism — a development strategy*

Rural Development Commission, English Tourist Board, Countryside Commission (1991) *The green light: A guide to sustainable tourism*

Wales Tourist Board (1988) *Tourism in Wales — developing the potential*

Recreation and access

Countryside recreation is enjoyed by all age groups and is increasing in popularity. Passive and active forms of recreation will be commonplace in all of the AONBs and, in many cases, may be substantially absorbed without damage to the environment. Although providing for recreation is not a primary purpose of AONBs, the increasing demands placed upon these areas for various forms of recreation and for increased access need to be planned for through the management plan. The management plan is the vehicle for helping to resolve conflicts of use and environmental problems that may arise from recreational activity, and for promoting compatible recreational activities.

The principal recreational pursuits, their current and potential levels of participation and the distribution of activity need to be established and assessed in terms of the actual and potential impact on the environment, and on other users and activities within the AONB.

The policies of the plan should seek to resolve any conflicts that have been identified, but at the same time also seek to maximise recreational opportunities where they are compatible with the primary aim of conserving natural beauty. They should be strategic in nature and should reflect other strategic priorities identified in statutory or non-statutory plans for areas wider than the AONB. Detailed proposals should be covered in the zone-based section of the plan.

Particular importance should be attached to management of the public rights of way network and in meeting the target of the end of the century set by the Commission by which time the network should be legally defined, properly maintained and signposted, and well publicised. A target of 1995 has since been set in Wales by the Council.

References and sources of information

The promotion and/or management of recreational activity and access opportunities within AONBs will be the concern of many organisations. These include the local planning authorities, Sports Council, Sports Council for Wales, Countryside Commission, English Nature, Countryside Council for Wales and a variety of amenity and conservation groups. Information on the existing and potential recreational or access opportunities and their impact on other interests may be obtained from these sources.

Countryside Commission (1989) *Enjoying the countryside: Priorities for action*, CCP 235
Countryside Commission (1989) *Horses in the countryside*, CCP 261
Countryside Commission (1989) *Managing rights of way: An agenda for action*, CCP 273
Countryside Commission (1989) *Paths, routes and trails: Policies and priorities*, CCP 266
Countryside Commission (1989) *Policies for enjoying the countryside*, CCP 234
Countryside Commission (1991) *Visitors to the countryside*, CCP 341
Sidaway, R. (1988) *Sport, recreation and nature conservation*, Sports Council
Sports Council (1991) *Good practice for sport and recreation*
Tourism and Recreation Research Unit (1983) *Recreation site survey manual*, E & F N Spon

Traffic management and car parking

These subjects are closely related to tourism and recreation provision and may not warrant a separate section of the plan. However in AONBs that are subject to large visitor pressures it may be necessary to separate out the impact of vehicles from the other issues that arise from these activities.

The main issues that are likely to arise include congestion of road networks, indiscriminate parking, visual intrusions and noise, and physical erosion or damage.

A better appreciation of the problems and possible solutions can be gained by the collation of data on vehicle numbers, and movements, diurnal and seasonal patterns, trends, bottlenecks and other problem areas, for example. Objectives and policies should be aimed at reducing these conflicts but only where such measures would be compatible with conservation requirements. For instance, road widening or extra parking provision would be unacceptable in many situations and a preferred approach may be the improvement of public transport services to reduce overall traffic volumes linked with the introduction of park and ride schemes. The provision of a better rural transport network will also have benefits for the local community and may be supported by the Rural Development Commission under their rural transport support schemes.

The *Gower management plan* includes the following typical traffic management objectives:

2.77 Road improvements will only be carried out for reasons of safety and where traffic management measures are inadequate.

2.78 To resist additional parking in areas of severe visitor pressure.

2.79 To promote well-designed small-scale car parks for low-key countryside recreation at appropriate locations.

2.80 To consider provision of an early warning system of traffic congestion and to seek coordination and dissemination of traffic information.

2.81 To take measures to prevent parking giving access to sensitive and fragile areas.

2.82 Indiscriminate parking will be discouraged where it intrudes or damages the landscape. Rationalisation of such parking will be promoted.

2.83 To promote improvements to the environmental quality of existing car parks.

2.84 To make greater use of car parks for the availability and location of information and interpretive material.

2.85 To discuss with the public transport undertakings possible schemes for improved and specialised bus services to the area.

References

Countryside Commission (1981) *Recreational public transport*, Advisory Series No 5

Countryside Commission (1987) *Public transport to the countryside: A marketing handbook for operators and local authorities*, CCP 227

Rural Development Commission (undated) *Opportunities in rural transport*

Rural Development Commission (undated) *Rural transport problems*

Interpretation

Interpretation is a valuable means of raising awareness of the importance of AONBs and thus contributing to their enjoyment and successful conservation. It should include interpretation of the area's natural and cultural heritage, for residents, visitors and especially school children. It can also be a useful tool in influencing visitor patterns.

The management plan should consider the current level of interpretive provision and identify opportunities for its enhancement. Priority should be given to proposals that may help to resolve particular environmental problems or conflicts of use. Where individual projects relate to a specific area these should be described in the zone-based section of the plan. Where they are of a more general nature, or apply across the AONB, they can be described here. Many organisations are producing educational and interpretive material. The Plan can help avoid unnecessary duplication of effort.

References and sources of information

Sources of information on techniques for countryside interpretation and the current level of provision within an AONB will include the Countryside Commission, English Nature, Countryside Council for Wales, Forestry Commission, the Centre for Environmental Interpretation at Manchester Polytechnic, local authorities and local conservation bodies.

Aldridge, D. (1975) *Guide to countryside interpretation. I: Principles of countryside interpretation and interpretative planning*, HMSO, Edinburgh

Countryside Commission (1977) *Interpretative planning*, Advisory Series No.2

Grater, R. (1976) *The interpreters handbook*, S.W. Parks and Monuments Trust

Millman, R. & Young, B. (1984) *Planning for interpretation*, CEI

Pennyfather, K. (1975) *Guide to countryside interpretation II: Interpretative media and facilities*, HMSO, Edinburgh

Tilden, F. (1977) (rev. edn) *Interpreting our heritage*, University of North Carolina Press

Yates, F.N. (1985) *Natural history teaching resources*, Ecological Parks Trust

Settlement and community

Control of new development within villages and settlements is principally a function of the statutory planning system. However, the management plan offers an opportunity for a broader look at the social needs of the community. For example, the plan may provide guidance on the siting and design of farm buildings and may describe how rural housing or other development may be reconciled with conservation objectives.

The assessment of landscape character and quality will provide guidance on the suitability, scale and appearance of development within the context of different landscape types. Principles of location and design may also be established, which can be used to guide assessment of individual development proposals.

In suitable areas, appropriate development may be positively encouraged where it helps to bring services to rural areas or assists in sustaining and developing rural communities. The plan should indicate the types of development that may be encouraged and potential sources of assistance, such as grant aid and advice from the Rural Development Commission, Welsh Development Agency or Development Board for Rural Wales.

References and sources of information
Relevant organisations include the Rural Development Commission, Welsh Development Agency, Development Board for Rural Wales, Countryside Commission, Countryside Council for Wales, Rural Community Councils and the Country Landowners' Association
Country Landowners' Association (1989) *Enterprise in the rural environment*
Department of the Environment/Welsh Office Planning Policy Guidance Notes (1992) *The countryside and the rural economy*, PPG 7 (draft)
English Heritage (1990) *Conversion of historic farm buildings*
Watkins, C. and Winter, M. (1988) *Superb conversions? farm diversification — the farm building experience*, Centre for Rural Studies and Council for the Protection of Rural England

Industrial development, road schemes and mineral workings

These subjects are also covered by statutory planning policies but the management plan can provide additional guidance on the relative sensitivity to development of different parts of the AONB and on measures that can be taken to mitigate the impact of past and potential developments of this kind.

Policies should seek to strengthen the case against potentially damaging developments and guide any other development pressures towards areas most able to accommodate them. Proposals may include management to reduce the impact on the landscape of past developments, such as mineral workings and highway schemes. Opportunities for enhancing the landscape or wildlife potential of abandoned mineral workings or other degraded areas should also be identified, and policies agreed for after uses.

Development objectives may typically include the following (taken from the *Clwydian Range AONB management plan*):

Development objectives

2.14.1 To seek to ensure that any development within the AONB is compatible with the aims of AONB designation.
2.14.2 To encourage high standards of improvement and alterations to properties and buildings reflecting the traditional rural character of the area.
2.14.3 To encourage sympathetic landscape proposals associated with all new developments in order to achieve harmony with the landscape.
2.14.4 To encourage high standards of design and landscaping in road improvement schemes.
2.14.5 To resist all proposals for new mineral workings within the AONB and to strive for landscaping and restoration of the highest quality where proposals for the extension of existing workings are considered acceptable.

4. ZONE STRATEGY AND PROPOSALS

Introduction

Although the strategic objectives and policies of the previous chapter provide a direction and framework for management within the AONB as a whole, they need to be applied to specific areas if they are to be successfully translated into action on the ground.

In the larger, or more complex AONBs this task is greatly simplified by dividing the area into more manageable tracts of countryside or **zones**. These zones may, for example, be based on landscape character areas, physical characteristics, patterns of use or geographical units related to parish or other such boundaries. Whatever the basis for zoning, however, the resulting areas should represent discrete and identifiable tracts of land within which the major management issues, objectives and priorities can be clearly identified.

Many existing plans adopt a zone-based approach, usually defined by the physical or land-use characteristics that give each area a different identity (eg *Mendip Hills local plan, Gower management plan*).

Other plans, particularly in coastal areas, adopt the zoning principles advocated by the Countryside Commission in the document *The coastal heritage* (1970), which suggest zonation according to levels of use under the broad headings of 'intensive', 'remote' and 'transitional' areas. The *Coastal management plan for the Isle of Anglesey*, for example, develops this system into a five-tier zonal classification, including 'sensitive' and 'promotional' with the above three.

Zone studies

Introduction

Each zone study should begin with a description of its individual features and characteristics, together with a summary of any relevant designations or other factors that may constrain or influence management opportunities. This information is usefully summarised in plan form.

Zone strategy

Discussion of the main issues and priorities for management within the zone leads on to the establishment of an overall zone management strategy. This reflects the strategic objectives and policies identified for the AONB as a whole but applies and includes only those that are relevant to the characteristics and issues particular to that zone.

Action requirements and proposals

Within the framework of zone management priorities, individual action requirements and proposals can then be identified for specific sites or areas. It may be helpful to consider the action requirements under relevant subject headings (eg landscape, nature conservation, cultural heritage, recreation, tourism etc) allowing cross-reference to be made to wider AONB objectives and policy. Priorities and lead agencies for implementation should be identified against each proposal where possible.

The proposals will form the basis of annual work programmes, which will be produced separately from the main plan and will detail individual projects or tasks against a time-scale, a financial allocation and an implementing body. The proposals should be set out in the management plan in such a way that this link is easily made, for example by setting out a schedule of proposals with reference codes that can be directly related to work programme tasks.

eg The proposals identified for Zone A could be itemised as follows:

Zone A proposals

A1 Recreation and tourism

A1.1 Footpath improvements at x location

A1.2 Provision of new picnic site at x location etc

and can be translated into work programme tasks using the same reference code system:

Work programme Zone A

A1.1 Footpath improvements at x location

A1.1 a Cut back encroaching vegetation along footpath length

b Erect stile at x location

c Footpath resurfacing

d Erect fingerpost signs at x locations etc

Arrangements for work programming are discussed further in chapter 5.

5. IMPLEMENTING THE PLAN

Putting the plan into practice requires:

- the support and participation of landowners, local authorities, public agencies, voluntary bodies, private organisations and individuals;
- sufficient financial resources to fund programmes of work on the ground, and other land management initiatives;
- a willingness of all concerned to work together towards agreed objectives.

It is important therefore to identify in this Chapter:

- who will participate in implementing the plan;
- how policy and implementation proposals will be organised and managed,
    - —what resources are needed (in terms of manpower, finance, equipment etc);
- sources of financial support,
    - —programming the work;
- how the completed implementation plans are to be monitored, evaluated and reviewed.

Participants

This section should describe what local authority staff resources are available for project implementation, any training required, and the need to harness and coordinate the activities of a wide range of organisations and individuals through cooperation and commitment to agreed management policies.

Policy implementation by local authorities

The role of local authorities should be identified in assisting the implementation of management plan policies through various statutory functions, especially development control powers, and advising on policy formulation and review through the JAC.

Project implementation by local authorities

The role of local authorities in the direct implementation of projects or management activities should be reviewed, including the activities undertaken by countryside management services and ranger services. This section should also consider the role of local authorities as agents for the Commission and the Council in implementing projects, for example through landscape conservation grants, and the provision of grants by local authorities themselves to support management activities by others.

The role of other public bodies

Reference is made here to the contribution that other public bodies can make to implementing the plan such as English Nature, English Heritage, Cadw, Forestry Commission, MAFF, Welsh Office Agriculture Department, National Rivers Authority etc.

The role of voluntary bodies, private organisations and individuals

It is important to recognise the existing and potential contribution that voluntary bodies and particularly private individuals as landowners make to AONB management. Those bodies with a direct management role have been described earlier but note should be made of other 'umbrella' organisations (eg CPRE, CPRW, CLA, NFU, FUW etc) that should be involved in the consultative process because of the influence they may have on public opinion generally and on those directly engaged in management activity.

Organisation and management

The management plan should describe the mechanisms proposed for the coordination of the multiplicity of relevant interest groups. If one does not exist already, it may recommend the establishment of a JAC or similar forum, and explain its role and the proposed representation and consultative mechanisms. The need for the nomination of an officer at senior level to coordinate the planning and implementation of management and act as a focal point within the AONB administrative framework should be stressed. This officer should hold a senior permanent position and be able to devote an adequate proportion of his/her time to AONB duties. The creation of a specialist management unit may be recommended. The training needs of those involved with AONB management, including JAC members, should also be considered and a programme of training outlined.

The AONB Officer would be primarily responsible for providing the JAC with information in draft form regarding the organisation and management of implementation proposals. These should be discussed, amended if necessary, and approved by the JAC. A schedule should be prepared that clearly identifies the lead agency responsible for implementing policy and the role of supporting organisations. Procedures for consultation should also be set out so that a broad spectrum of 'ownership' will be obtained.

It may be appropriate to establish a separate forum for consultation composed of representatives of amenity bodies and individuals, that meets the JAC once or twice a year.

The terms of reference and composition of a Consultative Bodies Group, if deemed necessary, should be established in this section.

The JAC for the Quantock Hills is advised by a group of interested bodies that meets at regular intervals. An extract is included from the *Quantock Hills management plan* to illustrate the composition of the Consultative Bodies Group.

The consultative bodies

There is a need to ensure that all of the consultative bodies involved have a direct interest and knowledge of Quantock affairs — otherwise they cannot make a meaningful contribution to discussion. As is made clear in Section 18 of the plan, there is a continuing need for all groups who wish to use the hills for an event to inform the Warden in advance to ensure there is no conflict of use. Since the draft plan was published the Joint Liaison Group has carried out a detailed review of the consultative bodies and as a result removed a number of bodies who either made little contribution or who had satisfactory contact with the Warden Service already. As a result the Consultative Bodies Group, who meet the Joint Liaison Group once or twice a year, consists of representatives of:

The Army
Bridgwater & District Civic Society
Community Council for Somerset
Council for the Protection of Rural England
Country Landowners' Association
Cyclists' Touring Club
Devon and Somerset Association for Deer Protection

40 Commando, Royal Marines
Forestry Commission
Friends of Quantock
The Girl Guides
Great Wood Camp
League Against Cruel Sports
Leonard Wills Field Centre
Ministry of Agriculture Fisheries & Food
National Farmers' Union
National Trust
Nature Conservancy Council (now English Nature)
Quantock Commoners' Association
Quantock Pony Breeders' Association
Quantock Riding Centre
Quantock Society
Quantock Staghounds
Somerset Area Ramblers' Association
Somerset Archaeological & Natural History Society
Somerset Association of Local Councils
Somerset County Council Education Department
Somerset County Scout Council
Somerset Trust for Nature Conservation
Trail Riders Fellowship
Voluntary Warden Service
West Bagborough Residential Centre
West Country Tourist Board
West Somerset Bridleways Association
Youth Hostels' Association

Resources required

It is first necessary to identify, in general terms, the resources required to implement the plan — these will include resources of manpower, equipment and finance — and the potential contribution of different groups. This will enable resources to be sought, and a phased plan for implementation prepared though annual work programmes.

Sources of finance

Public sector funding

The various sources of public sector funding should be briefly described. These will include grants or funds obtained from local authorities, Department of Environment, Countryside Commission, Countryside Council for Wales, English Nature, European Community, Rural Development Commission, Welsh Development Agency, Development Board for Rural Wales, Sports Councils for England and Wales, English and Wales Tourist Boards, English Heritage, Cadw, MAFF, Welsh Office Agricultural Department, etc.

Joint Advisory Committees at present do not normally raise their own sources of finance but receive a contribution to fund a management service from county and district council sources. As a large majority of AONBs are located in rural areas where there are often competing demands for limited council resources, JACs usually receive a relatively small contribution of a few thousand pounds from each authority. Although this level of finance may be matched by the Commission or the Council, the total available in each year is normally insufficient to meet the requirements of financing staff and carrying out even modest work on the ground.

The degree to which these resources are exploited should be discussed and opportunities for improving the financial arrangements identified. This may involve joint budgeting, tapping new funds, partnership arrangements, or a wider application of financial incentives from other organisations, for example through the Countryside Stewardship scheme.

The contribution of the private/voluntary sector

The voluntary sector will have little in the way of financial resources to spare for management work but may be able to make a significant contribution to the management effort in kind, particularly as a source of manpower. Voluntary work parties, organised by such bodies as the National Trust, County Wildlife Trusts and the British Trust for Conservation Volunteers for example, can achieve

significant results. The management plan should acknowledge this contribution in any assessment of available resources.

Likewise, individual landowners also contribute 'in kind' by carring out work on their own land in accordance with the Plan's objectives.

In some AONBs possibilities may exist for raising additional finance from private sources. These may include private estates or local industrial concerns who may be able to sponsor environmental work to improve their 'green' image and demonstrate concern for the environment. In general, this source of income is not common, nor can it be relied upon, and it must be regarded as secondary to the local government contribution and the Commission or the Council grants. However, local authorities should be encouraged to investigate as broad a range of funding possibilities as possible.

Opportunities also exist for the achievement of plan objectives through conditional exemption from Inheritance Tax where the conservation agencies advise the Capital Taxes Office on qualifying land and on the management arrangements that should apply.

Budgeting and financial monitoring

The financial implications of the plan policies should be discussed and related to likely contributions identified in the previous sections.

An estimate of annual income and expenditure should be prepared to identify the finance available to support a programme of implementation work.

Expenditure items should include permanent staff costs (or the cost of seconded local authority staff). Overheads for the technical input by local authority staff, including printing of plans, and general administrative assistance are usually absorbed by the local authorities but this contribution should be noted. Other expenditure items could be grouped under sub-headings such as: Countryside Implementation Service, Information, Conservation Projects, Training and Administration.

Annual income should be assessed. This is likely to be made up of:

- local authority contributions;

- grant aid;

- profit from sale of leaflets and other publications;

- subscriptions, gifts or sponsorship from industry, residents or visitors;

- advertising, paying events, guided walks.

An income and expenditure account should be drawn up to show the anticipated budget figures. These can then be compared at the end of prescribed periods, usually quarterly, with the actual or committed amounts.

A more complete set of costs need to be produced after the management plan implementation programme has been 'up and running' for an adequate length of time. This will provide information for use in preparing a 'business plan' to give potential sponsors information on the possible value for money that investment in the AONB may yield. It will also provide a means of measuring the efficiency of the implementation work and demonstrate the level of external support received.

Implementation programmes that include specific tasks also need to be budgeted for, and their costs continually monitored against estimates to ensure that funds are controlled. Allocating finances to work programmes and the process of monitoring and review of management plan proposals are considered in the next sections.

Work programmes

Although the work programmes themselves will be produced as separate documents from the management plan, in order to facilitate more regular up-date and review, the plan should make reference to work programming arrangements.

The plan will have identified a large number of proposals for action, which will help to achieve short- and long-term management objectives. The implementation of these proposals will depend upon the available resources in any one year and choices will have to be made between projects for inclusion in annual work programmes. These choices should reflect the priorities indicated by the plan but will also inevitably reflect a reaction to opportunities, available at that time, where advantage can be taken of offers of manpower or financial resources for specific projects.

Provisional work programmes for years two and three or beyond may also be drafted to assist in financial planning and bids for resources beyond the current financial year. For example, the Commission or the Council may be able to guarantee funding for management work for five to six years against an agreed programme of action.

Individual projects and tasks should be itemised and cross-referenced to the relevant proposal within the management plan. Estimated costs at current prices should be indicated and, where relevant, the type of expenditure, ie capital or revenue. Likely contributors to these costs and responsibility for implementation should also be indicated against each task, together with a level of priority. A range of sources of finance can be tapped and the identification of tasks and priorities can help to target these resources to the most important areas, as well

as provide the basis on which to bid for extra funds or enter agreements over joint funding. Wherever possible, targets and performance indicators should be identified against specific projects to act as the basis for future monitoring.

Monitoring and review

The importance of monitoring and review is generally recognised as an essential part of the management planning process but it is rarely described in any detail within existing plans. The levels at which monitoring is to be undertaken, the procedures and frequency of review, and with whom the responsibility lies for carrying it out, all need to be established clearly at the outset. A general statement of intention to 'monitor progress' is not enough. Four main levels of monitoring should be considered.

Monitoring progress within the annual work programme

A half-yearly review of progress and spend, with a full review at the year end, is considered to be the minimum requirement. The results of this exercise will assist in the review of plans and priorities for the following year, carrying over, if necessary, projects that have not been completed within the programme.

Identifying how management effort has been targeted

When drawing up the work programme for the following year a quick review can be made of the spread of management activity against the proposals and priorities of the plan. If one area of management has received particular attention to date but another priority area has been neglected, for example, the balance can be redressed in the coming year. Priorities may also have changed within the year and this annual review will allow adjustments to be made in the targeting of management to the areas of greatest need.

Assessing the effectiveness of this action in relation to achieving plan objectives

This should include a re-assessment of the overall direction and strategy of the plan in the light of changing circumstances. This will require a reassessment of the condition of the AONB and of the major issues affecting it, taking into account the effects of ongoing management and changing external influences. Depending upon the time-scale chosen for this review there may be no need to modify the overall strategic objectives of the plan, which will remain relevant over the next plan period. The priorities may change, however, in response to the changing political or socio-economic climate, and proposals for management may need to be adjusted to take account of work already implemented or new opportunities that have arisen over the plan period. A major review of this nature could not be undertaken within an interval of less than 5 years.

It may be desirable in some cases to link the major review cycle to those of the relevant statutory plans. This would maximise opportunities for feedback from the management plan review to be accommodated within the review of local planning policy, and vice versa. In practice, and particularly in multi-county AONBs, such close coordination may not be feasible and a certain degree of independence from the statutory plan system may be viewed as desirable in maintaining the principle of collective ownership of the management plan.

Developing output measures for monitoring at a national level

Finally, the information that any major review of the condition of the AONB will provide will also be of great value to the Commission and the Council at a national level, in their bids for funding and in targeting extra resources towards areas of greatest need. Discussions with the Commission or the Council will be necessary in order to devise output measures that are of greatest relevance to a strategic overview of the condition of AONBs in general. A review statement outlining progress over the plan period would be produced as a separate document alongside the revision of the management plan.

Responsibilities and procedures

Monitoring at these various levels has quite considerable resource implications that must be identified as part of the plan in order that adequate time and money are allocated to this essential element of the management planning process. It is necessary to be as clear as possible with regard to who will be involved at each level of monitoring, how long the exercise is likely to take, and what is actually involved in the process.

The annual work programme review is a relatively straightforward task, comprising a statement of progress and spend, and a brief examination of the priorities and opportunities for implementation in the coming year. The five-yearly plan review is a totally different scale of exercise, however, and a major resource commitment will need to be planned for in order to undertake the task. As a very rough guide, the requirements are likely to be similar to those employed in the preparation of the original plan.

REFERENCES

Anglesey Borough Council (1982) *A coastal management plan for the Isle of Anglesey.*

Avon and Somerset County Councils (1989) *Mendip Hills local plan.*

Clwyd County Council (1988) *Clwydian Hills management plan.*

Clwydian Range AONB Joint Advisory Committee (1989) *The Clwydian Range AONB management plan.*

Countryside Commission (1970) *The coastal heritage,* HMSO.

Countryside Commission (1986) *Management plans,* CCP 206

Countryside Commission (1991) *Areas of Outstanding Natural Beauty: A policy statement 1991,* CCP 356

Countryside Commission *et al.* (1989) *Blackdown Hills AONB draft statement of intent.*

Dedham Vale Joint Advisory Committee (1991) *The Dedham Vale and Stour Valley countryside project management plan.*

East and West Sussex County Councils (1986) *Sussex Downs AONB statement of intent.*

East Sussex, West Sussex, Surrey and Kent County Councils (1988) *High Weald AONB joint statement* (1st revision).

Lancashire County Council (1985) *Forest of Bowland AONB statement of intent.*

Smart, Prof G. and Anderson, Dr M. (1990) *Planning and Management of Areas of Outstanding Natural Beauty,* CCP 295, Countryside Commission

Somerset County Council (1989) *Quantock Hills management plan: Phase 1 proposals.*

Swansea City Council (1990) *Gower management plan.*

Warwickshire County Council (1990) *Arden landscape guidelines.*